Reclaiming My Stolen Ideas

Artist, Activist, Author Addie Marie Jones is the single
mother of three sons. Retired from the Seattle Police
Department Crime Prevention Division she resides in
Seattle. She has a Bachelor of Arts Degree in Com-
munications from the University of Washington and
a Certificate in Computer Graphics and Animation
from Bellevue College. Plus enough updated computer credits from Shoreline Community College to
qualify for yet another Certificate. She is now publish-
ing her own eBooks online..

....p 8

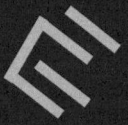

I NAMED GOOGLE — ADDIE'S ART BOOK YELLS is an

Ode to

My Crazy Imagination

ADDIE MARIE JONES

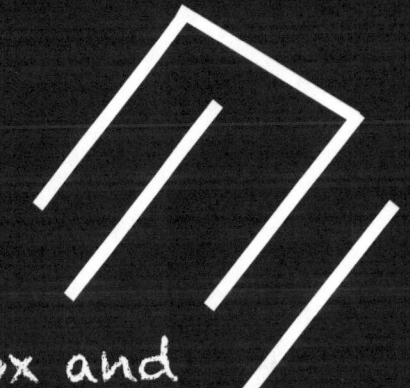

I think way outside the box and all around and upside down it too!

Education, my imagination and my children have been my salvation!

I LOVE everything computers! I even took a class punching wholes in cards at the old Edison Tech before it became Seattle Central Community College; before computers caught up to my imagination and got to now!

I'm telling my story because it's mine to tell; my unfortunate truth.

I've marched, I've door-belled, I've phone called for cause after cause upon cause. And I've community organized for years for Seattle Police Department Crime Prevention and gotten little to no credit for my work/suggestions so now I'm telling my own story here for somebody to listen to. Perhaps you!

Over the years I've suggested that "They"...use federal census tract boundaries in order to make police statistics meaningful and uniform. "They" implemented this. I suggested that "They"... monitor proposed legislation that affects African Americans and the poor then lobby proactively instead of reactively for changes in Olympia like the Welfare Rights Organizing Committee I volunteered with does...and "They (NAACP) implemented African American Legislative Day whereby busloads of community leaders lobby in Olympia every February after the session begins. Etcetera...   ...p. 13.

VISIONARY
OR ART BRUT

[Renditions from an upcoming children's book] This painting:

"Brown Faces" won inclusion in the Art & Literary Journal: Spindrift 2013 of Shoreline Community College, page 57.

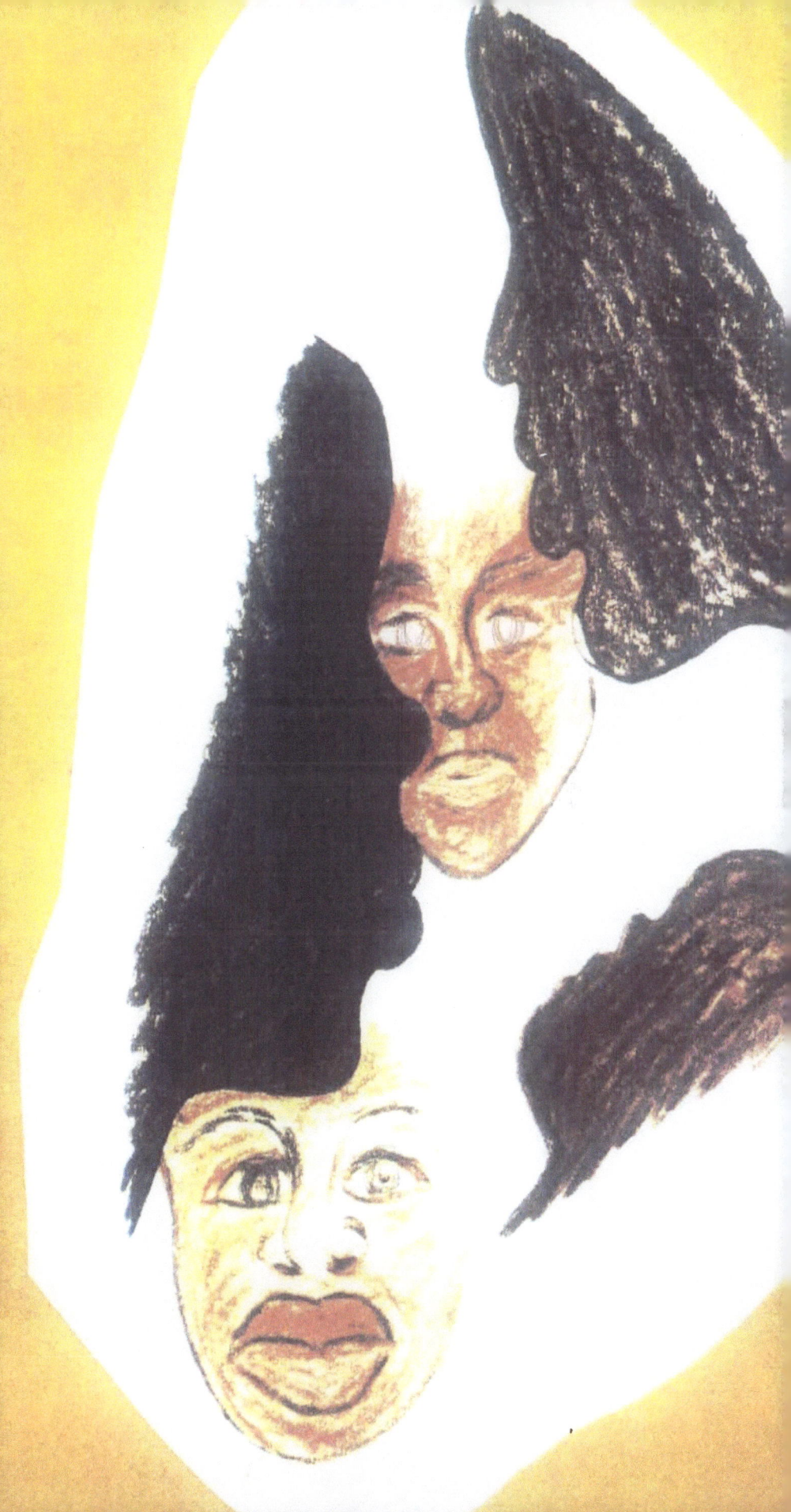

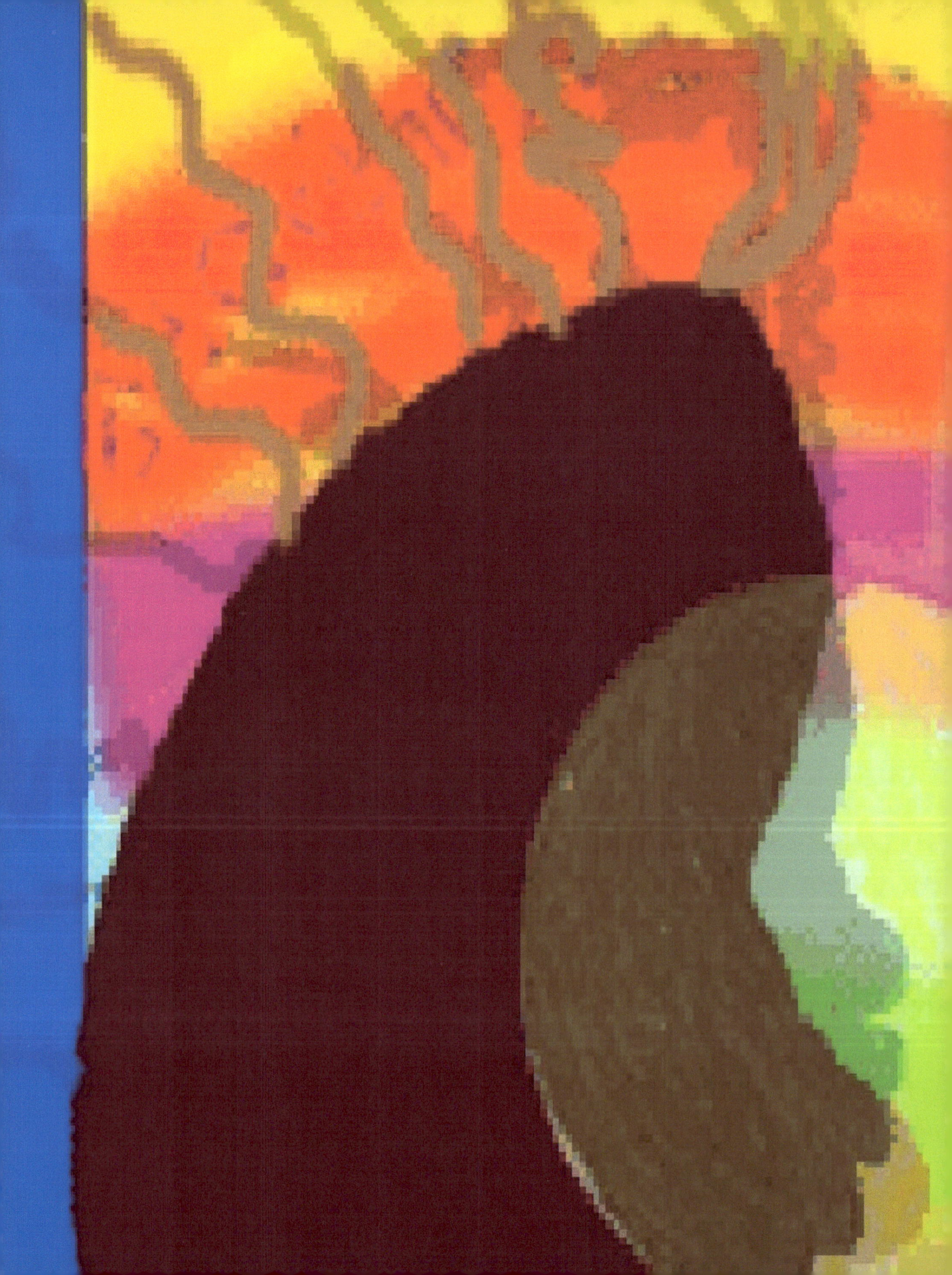

MORE VISIONARY
OR ART BRUT

[Renditions from
an upcoming
children's eBoook:
"Skin in The Game
...Color Me Proud"]

p 7 "There's a rainbow of
skin colored shades and
hues...
p 8 "Ethnic Sunshine"
p 10 "There's even Oreo
and Zebra Color too!"
p 11 "Night Sun"

9

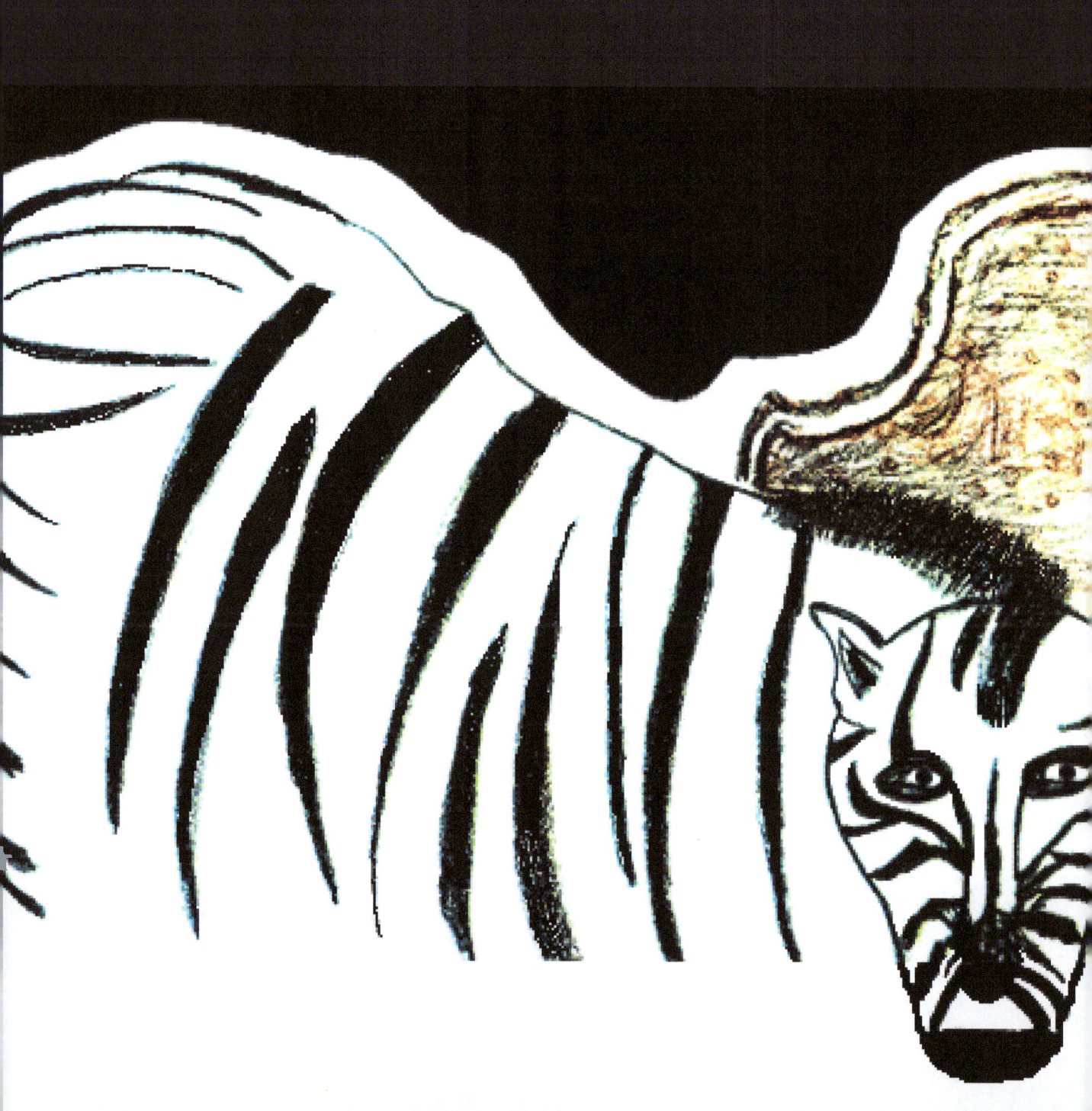

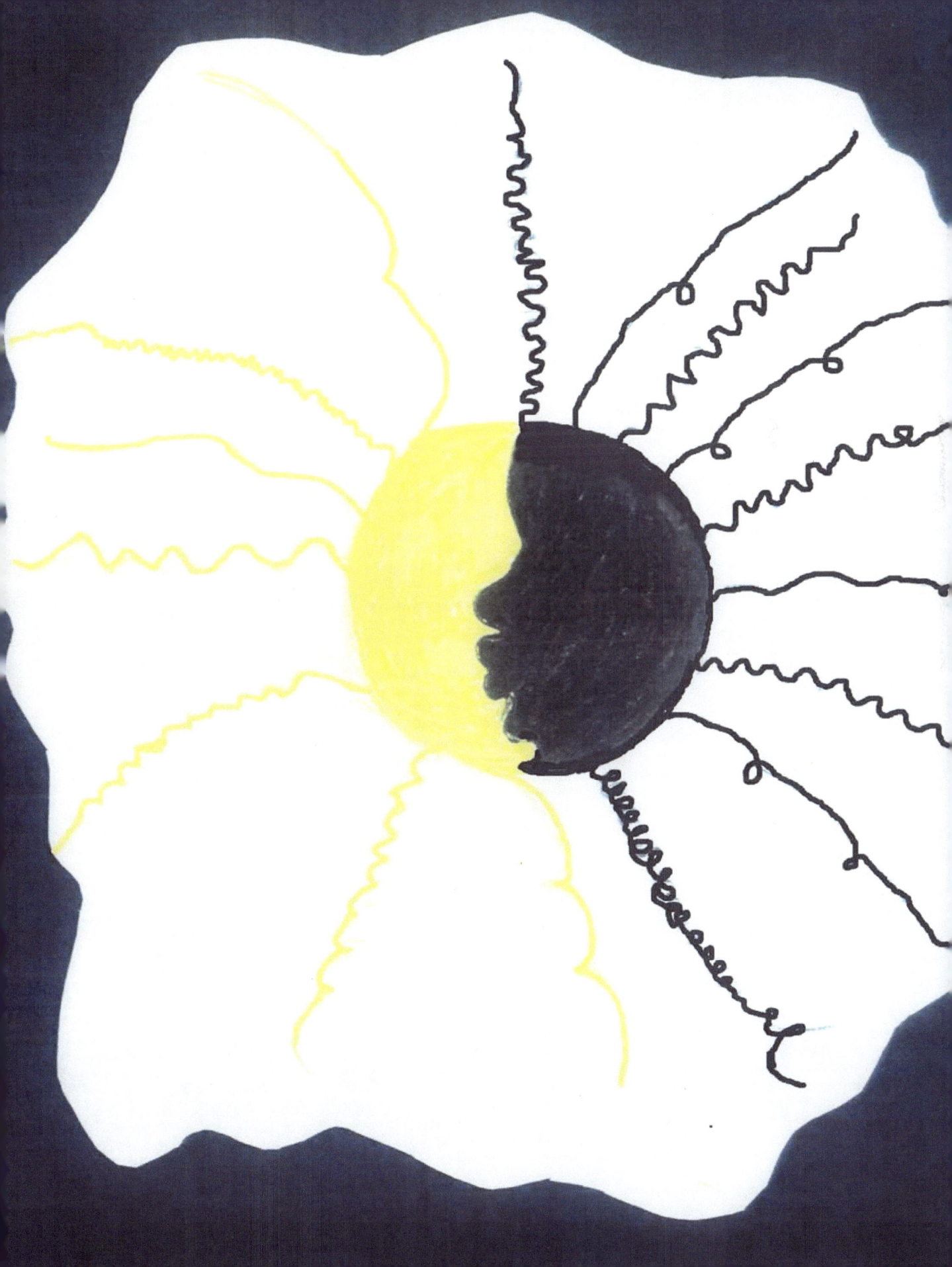

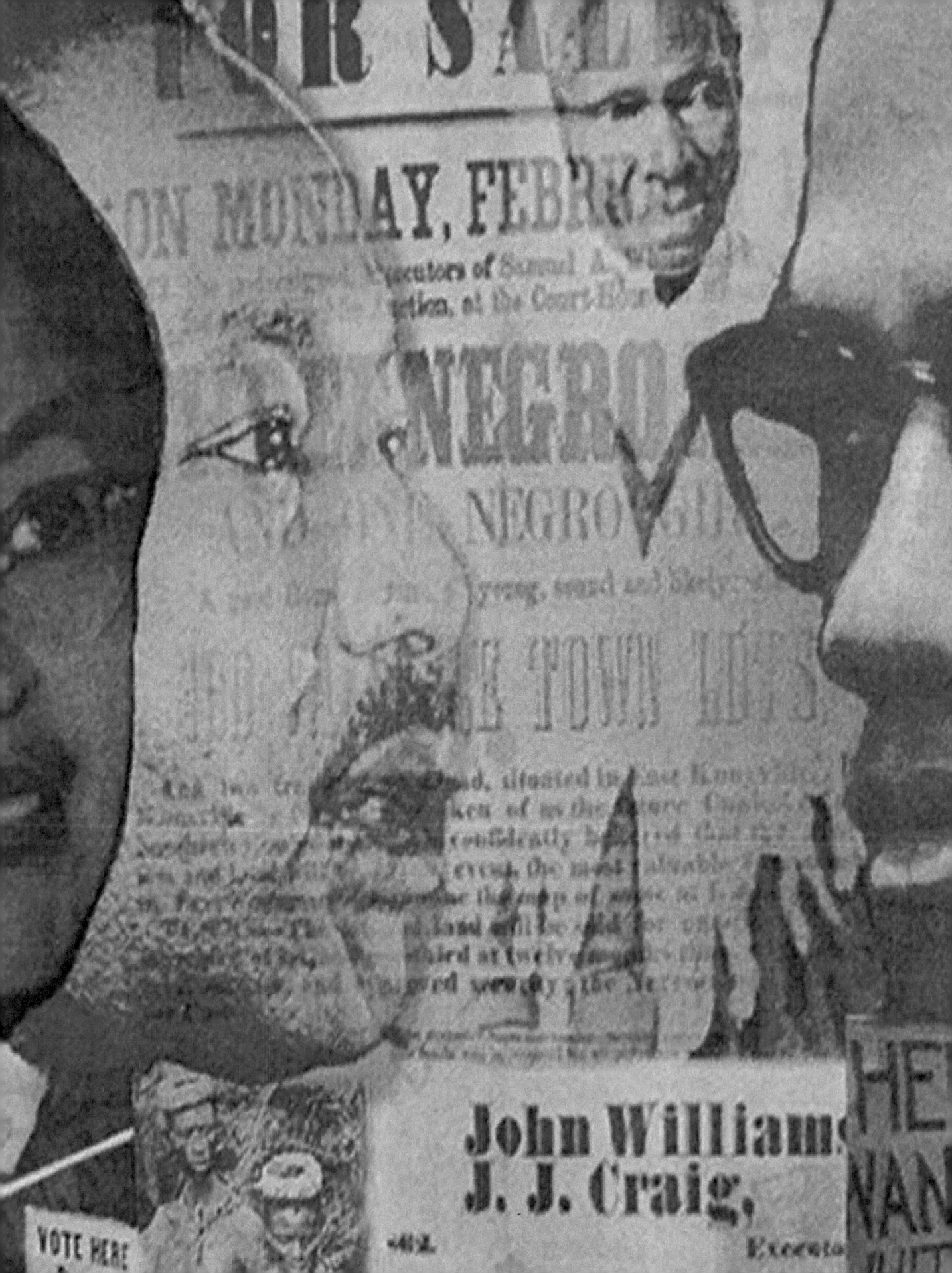

"Great Googly-Woogly" this turn of phrase should have netted me enough money to support my entire family and all my seven siblings' families for the rest of our lives (and for me not to be homeless for a while) if the founders of Google had lived up to their promise and the note they signed promising to pay me millions when they asked me if they could use this word – Google – to name their company and what this word means. Oodles and oodles, lots and lots I told them. I met and chatted with Serge Brin and Larry Page in the 90's outside a "How-To-Build-A-Business-On-The-Internet Seminar" in Bellevue. Very excited about Internet opportunities/possibilities I made the above exclamation when stating what a humongous business this would be – helping people find things on the Internet. I told them that Microsoft would probably develop this...

...Collage
Homage: to
Our Work History

And likely I saved Steve Jobs' job and his ass! (Apple had temporarily ousted him.) A teacher at my son's elementary school set up my meeting with Jobs. He put on a presentation at my son's school about the future of computers. I had all kinds of ideas about what computers could and should do. I guess word about me—a crazy black lady with whatever issue they tagged me with—had gotten out from all the Internet seminars, workshops and Focus Group meetings I somehow kept getting invited to.

Nothing was coincidental I now know. p 16

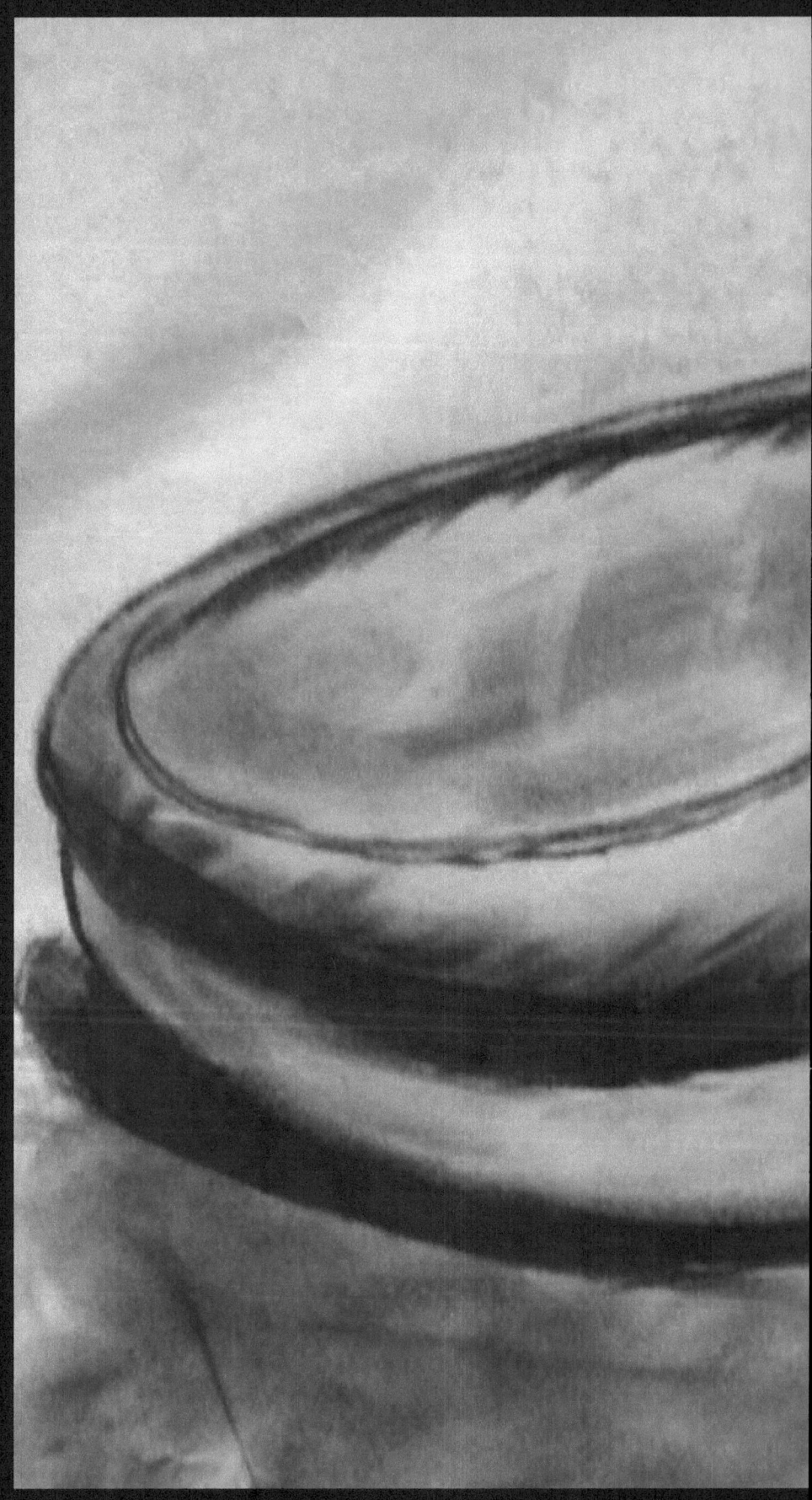

YOUR HATERS ARE
YOUR ELEVATORS

Pencil Drawing:
Walking in my
Shoes

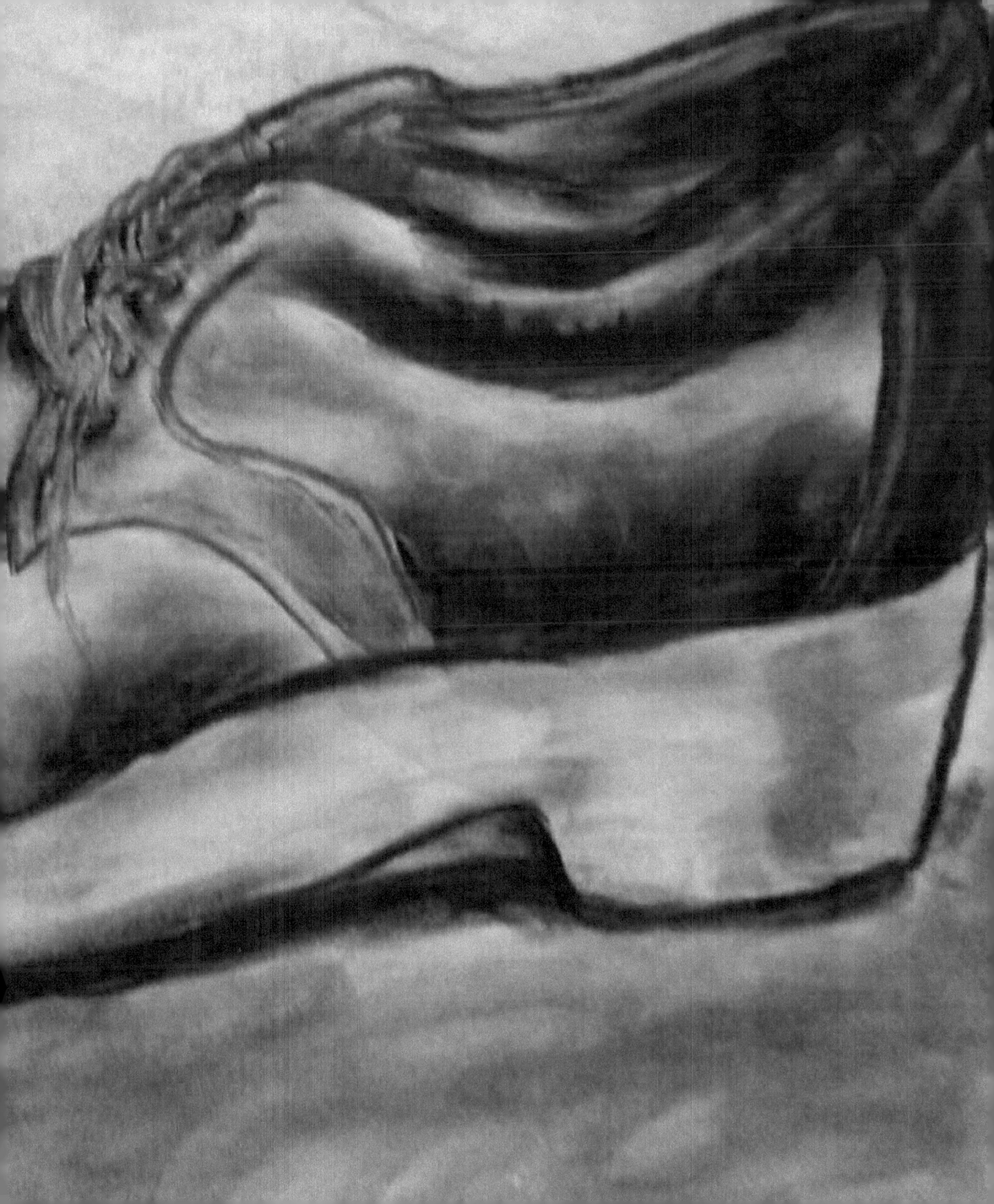

A Cold Fusion presentation impressed me most back then. And for $700 I bought a cable box to get the Internet on my TV.

Finally now computers can do (most of) what I imagined and envisioned in my head back then that I kept confusing with what I wanted to do on computers myself. But in actuality these programs/functions had not even been invented yet.

Since I was a little girl, late 49 early 50's, and saw my first television cartoons I dreamed them in color and saw words (I wanted to read or just watch) scrolling around on the screen flying, whirling, crawling, turning upside down, doing flips, jumping out of the TV in 3D all sorts of things. I guess I envisioned the Internet way before it was discovered.

Jobs took his time putting away the equipment he had showed his presentation on waiting until almost everybody but that teacher and me and my baby boy had left. And then my son had to go to the bathroom.

Jobs told that teacher to take him. And when they returned Jobs gestured and I could see that teacher helping my son play with some toys in an adjacent room with the door left open. And then he grilled me for what felt like more than an hour. I told him the same things I had told other "teckys" at some of these meetings.

I told him I wanted a steno-tablet sized computer that I could draw on.

He kept "what-elseing" me about futuristic things. I told him I loved the Star Trek episode where humans could not figure out how the alien space ship landed. Or how it operated because there were no visible buttons or controls, everything was touch-screen and laser.

Cell phones had to be pocket sized I told him about this subject. Then everybody and their momma would want one. Not the big clunky things that existed then. It would be nice if they were more like the Phaser on Star Trek and could do multiple things: have a camera, get the internet, show TV, movies, play music, yes even games too etc. And I told him televisions' should be like pictures on the wall or part of the wall itself.

I told him I didn't think I would see human teleportation in my lifetime because we have not mastered quantum physics yet. And that I thought flying devices/cars had already been invented but were being suppressed.

He kept pressing and squeezing my imagination; 3D GPS was something police departments where I worked were beginning to use. I explained the 3D I envisioned—people viewing movies on cocktail tables like a geographic correct hologram in your home. It would be like capturing Leprechauns or having your own village of little people I told him something I always wanted to have as a child.

At least I got software at meetings where I knew I was meeting with Microsoft guys. I chose an advanced copy of Windows Vista the last time I knew I was meeting with them where I asked,

"Why can't you just save things on the Internet?" A question I had posed to others before. And "can I get credit for these ideas?" I think the guy in the little room with me had asked me something about saving space or saving docs capacity. This guy grilled me about gaming mostly. The only thing I could think to tell him was that people would love to see themselves their face on a character in these games to become part of these games themselves.

Jobs treated me like shit! I felt raped and thrown into a ditch along side some lonely country road after this interview. Clearly he had no intention of ever giving me any credit whatsoever for this very valuable information or even acknowledging that I existed!

If Jobs is a Creative Genius then ...

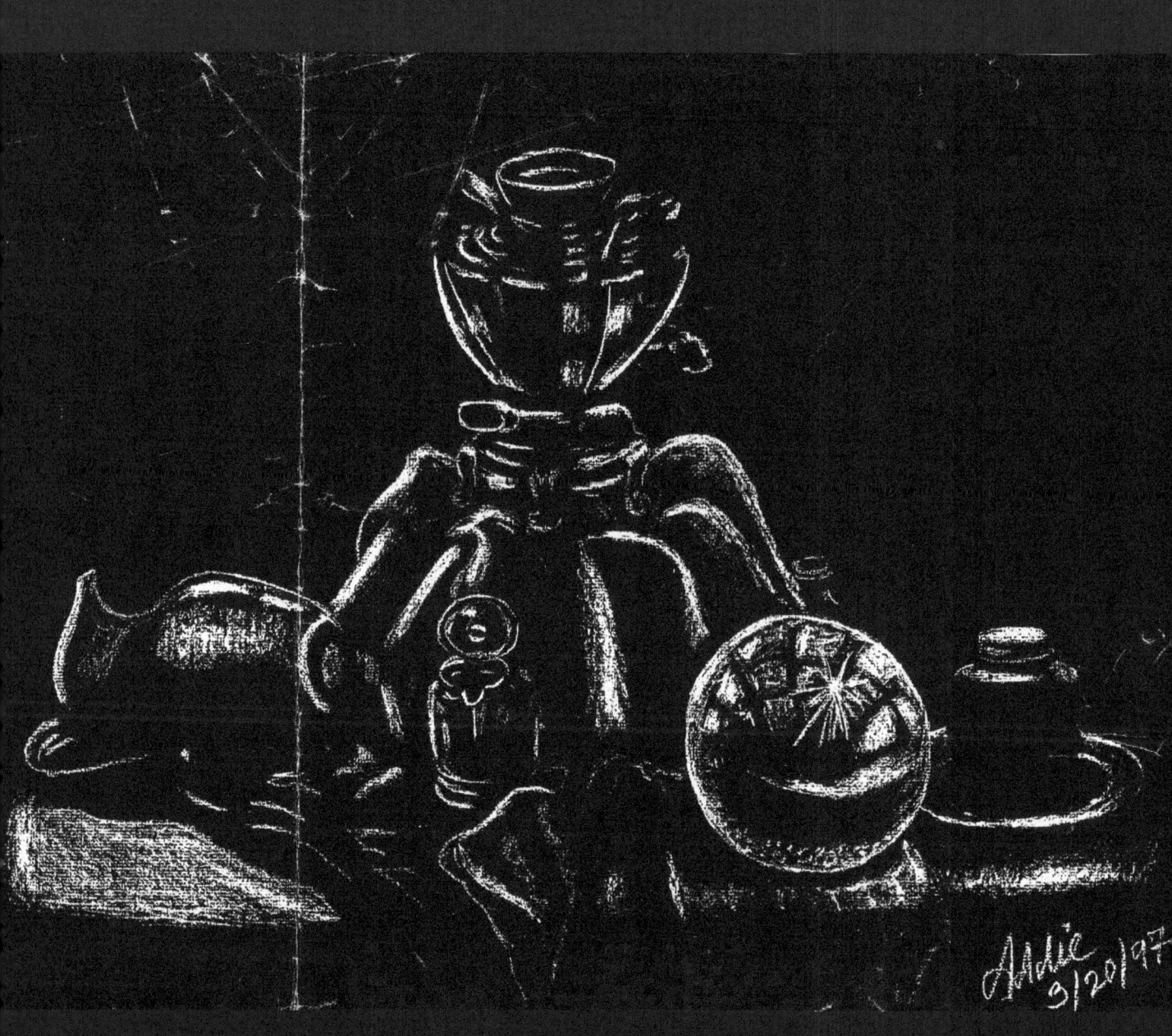

Addie
3/20/97

I sincere-
ly hope that
the Internet is the
Great Equalizer!

Help speak Truth to Power. TELL Google to pay me exactly what they promised!

Also ask Apple and Microsoft to match this amount so a $300 to $500 million dollar Small Business Development Fund can be established to reduce unemployment and build community in areas of high African American population concentration.

Perhaps it was in the late 80's and not the 70's, while working as a Program Coordinator for Seattle Police Crime Prevention, I gave one of my volunteer Block Captain's, Wanda Fullner who was working on her dissertation on micro-lending at Seattle University I think, paperwork detailing the Black Dollar Days Small Business Development Program run by Reverend Dr. Robert Jeffries. My son and I had enrolled in this program. She, and Peter Rose who was establishing a similar program in a Third World Country, used this to get grant funding to establish the Washington CASH (Community Alliance for Self Help) micro-lending Small Business Development Program here.

They quizzed and grilled me mercilessly to identify weaknesses in this program—follow-up and loan repayment I told them—and propose possible solutions. So they could build an improved more successful program model that would solve these problems.

Then later on in the 90's as a member myself of a Washington Cash Small Business Development Group, I showed Marcia Morningstar, she calls herself, who I thought was a friend, some ideas and graphic's I had written down about a newsletter I had named, Cash Notes, that would be perfect for Washington Cash. Immediately she told Cathy Gillman who headed this organization then. They started a newsletter with this name; I believe it is still online today.